Grade 1 Violin

Improve your sight-reading!

Paul Harris

D1328746

Extra Stage: Revision available to download from
fabermusicstore.com

FABER *ff* MUSIC

Introduction

Being a good sight-reader is so important and it's not difficult at all! If you work through this book carefully – always making sure that you really understand each exercise before you play it – you'll never have problems learning new pieces or doing well at sight-reading in exams!

Using the workbook

1 Rhythmic exercises
Make sure you have grasped these fully before you go on to the melodic exercises: it is vital that you really know how the rhythms work. There are a number of ways to do the exercises, several of which are outlined in Stage 1. Try them all out. Can you think of more ways to do them?

2 Melodic exercises
These exercises use just the notes (and rhythms) for the Stage, and are organised into Sets which progress gradually. If you want to sight-read fluently and accurately, get into the simple habit of working through each exercise in the following ways before you begin to play it:
- Make sure you understand the rhythm and counting. Clap the exercise through.
- Know what notes you are going to play and the fingering you are going to use.
- Try to hear the piece through in your head. Always play the first note to help.

3 Prepared pieces
Work your way through the questions first, as these will help you to think about or 'prepare' the piece. Don't begin playing until you are pretty sure you know exactly how the piece goes.

4 Going solo!
It is now up to you to discover the clues in this series of practice pieces. Give yourself about a minute and do your best to understand the piece before you play. Check the rhythms and fingering, and try to hear the piece in your head.

Always remember to feel the pulse and to keep going steadily once you've begun. Good luck and happy sight-reading!

Terminology:
Bar = measure

The golden rules

A sight-reading checklist

Before you begin to play a piece at sight, always consider the following:

1 Look at the piece for about half a minute and try to feel that you are *understanding* what you see (just like reading these words).

2 Look at the time signature and decide how you will count the piece.

3 Look at the key signature and think about how to finger the notes.

4 Notice patterns – especially those that repeat, or are based on scales and arpeggios.

5 Notice any markings that will help you convey the character.

6 Don't begin until you think you are going to play the piece accurately.

7 Count at least one bar in.

When performing a sight-reading piece

1 Keep feeling the pulse.

2 Keep going at a steady tempo.

3 Remember the finger pattern of the key you are in.

4 Ignore mistakes.

5 Look ahead – at least to the next note.

6 Play musically, always trying to convey the character of the music.

With many thanks to Gillian Secret for her invaluable help.

© 2011 by Faber Music Ltd
This edition first published in 2011 by Faber Music Ltd.
Bloomsbury House 74–77 Great Russell Street London WC1B 3DA
Music processed by Donald Thomson
Cover and page design by Susan Clarke
Cover illustration by Drew Hillier
Printed in England by Caligraving Ltd
All rights reserved

ISBN10: 0-571-53621-2
EAN13: 978-0-571-53621-4

US editions:
ISBN10: 0-571-53661-1
EAN13: 978-0-571-53661-0

Stage 1

D major $\frac{4}{4}$

Rhythmic exercises

The rhythmic exercises are really important. Always practise them carefully before going on. There are different ways of doing these exercises:

- Your teacher (or a metronome) taps the lower line while you clap or tap the upper line.
- You tap the lower line with your foot and clap or tap the upper line with your hands.
- You tap one line with one hand and the other line with the other hand on a table top.
- You tap the lower line and sing the upper line.

Before you begin each exercise count two bars in – one out loud and one silently.

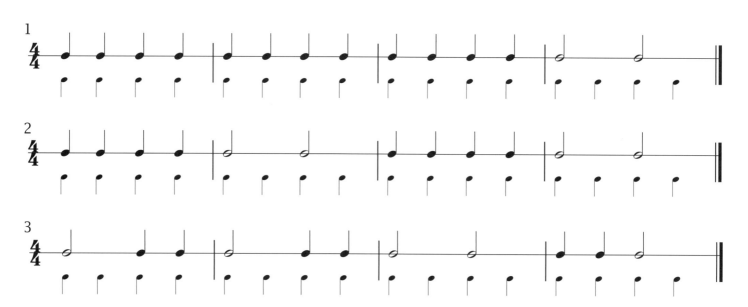

Melodic exercises

Set 1: Exploring the open D string

Hear each exercise in your head before you play it.

1

2

3

Set 2: Exploring the notes on the D string

Set 3: Exploring the D string notes plus open A string

Set 4: Exploring the D major scale

Prepared pieces

> **1** How many beats are there in each bar? What will you count?
>
> **2** What is the key? Play the scale.
>
> **3** What do bars 1 and 4, and bars 2 and 6 have in common?
>
> **4** Play a D (the first note), then hear the piece in your head.
>
> **5** How will you put some character into your performance?

> **1** How will you count this piece?
>
> **2** Tap the rhythm then, clapping the pulse, hear the rhythm silently in your head.
>
> **3** Are there any repeated rhythmic patterns?
>
> **4** Compare bar 1 with bar 4.
>
> **5** How will you put some character into your performance?

Improvising

> Make up your own piece (it can be as long or as short as you like), beginning with this pattern. Keep the pulse steady.
>
>
>
> Now make up your own piece in D major – using any notes of the scale you like.

Going solo!

Don't forget to prepare each piece carefully before you play it.

Stage 2

A major

Rhythmic exercises

Always remember to count two bars in.

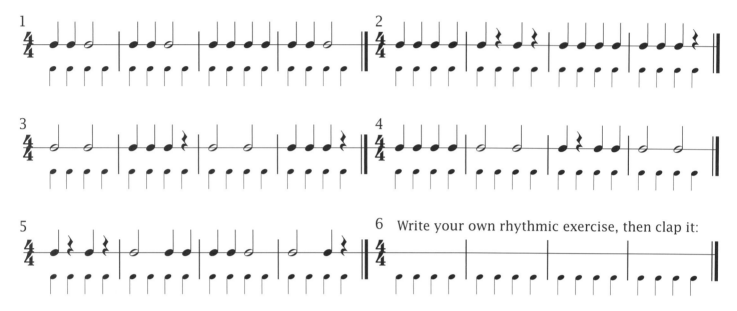

6 Write your own rhythmic exercise, then clap it:

Melodic exercises

Set 1: Exploring the first five notes of A major

Set 2: Exploring the A major scale

Set 3: Longer examples

Set 4: More crotchet rests

Prepared pieces

> **1** What is the key? Play the scale elegantly.
>
> **2** Tap the rhythm of the piece then hear the rhythm in your head.
>
> **3** Do any bars have the same rhythm?
>
> **4** Play an A (the first note) then hear the piece in your head.
>
> **5** How will you put character into your performance?

Elegantly

1

> **1** How will you finger the first note?
>
> **2** How are the first five bars similar?
>
> **3** What else do the first three bars have in common?
>
> **4** Tap the rhythm of the piece. Now hear the rhythm in your head.
>
> **5** How will you put some character into your performance?

Jokingly

2

Improvising

1

Make up your own piece (it can be as long or as short as you like), beginning with this pattern. Keep the pulse steady.

2

Now make up your own piece in A major – using any notes of the scale you like.

Going solo!

Don't forget to prepare each piece carefully before you play it.

Stage 3

Rhythmic exercises

Always remember to count two bars in.

Melodic exercises

Set 1: Exploring 3/4

Paul Harris' Exam Workout

Improve your sight-reading!

This best-selling series by renowned educationalist Paul Harris is designed to help incorporate sight-reading regularly into practice and lessons, and to prepare for the sight-reading test in grade examinations. The books offer a progressive series of enjoyable and stimulating stages which, with careful work, should result in considerable improvement from week to week.

ABRSM Editions

0-571-53300-0   Piano Pre-Grade 1
0-571-53301-9   Piano Grade 1
0-571-53302-7   Piano Grade 2
0-571-53303-5   Piano Grade 3
0-571-53304-3   Piano Grade 4
0-571-53305-1   Piano Grade 5
0-571-53306-X   Piano Grade 6
0-571-53307-8   Piano Grade 7
0-571-53308-6   Piano Grade 8

0-571-52405-2   Duets Grades 0–1
0-571-52406-0   Duets Grades 2–3

Trinity Editions

0-571-53750-2   Piano Grade Initial
0-571-53751-0   Piano Grade 1
0-571-53752-9   Piano Grade 2
0-571-53753-7   Piano Grade 3
0-571-53754-5   Piano Grade 4
0-571-53755-3   Piano Grade 5

0-571-53825-8   Electronic Keyboard Initial–Grade 1
0-571-53826-6   Electronic Keyboard Grades 2–3
0-571-53827-4   Electronic Keyboard Grades 4–5

Improve your sight-reading!
A piece a week   New

Two collections of fun, short pieces specifically written to be learnt one per week. This supports and improves sight-reading by developing note-reading skills and hand-eye coordination. By continually reading accessible new repertoire, the crucial processing of information is improved, developing confident sight-reading.

0-571-53937-8   A piece a week Grade 1
0-571-53938-6   A piece a week Grade 2

Improve your sight-reading!
Duets

Two graded duet books that give students a chance to practise their sight-reading skills alongside another player or teacher. Progressively paced to be used alongside the rest of the series.

0-571-52405-2   Grades 0–1
0-571-52406-0   Grades 2–3

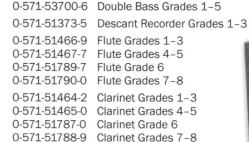

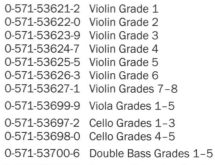

0-571-53621-2	Violin Grade 1
0-571-53622-0	Violin Grade 2
0-571-53623-9	Violin Grade 3
0-571-53624-7	Violin Grade 4
0-571-53625-5	Violin Grade 5
0-571-53626-3	Violin Grade 6
0-571-53627-1	Violin Grades 7–8
0-571-53699-9	Viola Grades 1–5
0-571-53697-2	Cello Grades 1–3
0-571-53698-0	Cello Grades 4–5
0-571-53700-6	Double Bass Grades 1–5
0-571-51373-5	Descant Recorder Grades 1–3
0-571-51466-9	Flute Grades 1–3
0-571-51467-7	Flute Grades 4–5
0-571-51789-7	Flute Grade 6
0-571-51790-0	Flute Grades 7–8
0-571-51464-2	Clarinet Grades 1–3
0-571-51465-0	Clarinet Grades 4–5
0-571-51787-0	Clarinet Grade 6
0-571-51788-9	Clarinet Grades 7–8
0-571-51635-1	Saxophone Grades 1–3
0-571-51636-X	Saxophone Grades 4–5
0-571-51633-5	Oboe Grades 1–3
0-571-57021-6	Oboe Grades 4–5
0-571-51148-1	Bassoon Grades 1–5
0-571-51076-0	Horn Grades 1–5
0-571-50989-4	Trumpet Grades 1–5
0-571-51152-X	Trumpet Grades 5–8
0-571-56860-2	Trombone Grades 1–5

Improve your aural!

The very thought of aural, especially in examinations, strikes fear into the heart of many young pianists and instrumentalists. But aural should not be an occasional optional extra – it's something to be developing all the time, because having a good ear will help improve musicianship more than any other single musical skill.

Improve your aural! is designed to take the fear out of aural. Through fun listening activities, boxes to fill in and practice exercises, these workbooks and CDs focus on all the elements of the ABRSM aural tests. Because all aspects of musical training are of course connected, the student will also be singing, clapping, playing their instrument, writing music down, improvising and composing – as well as developing that vital ability to do well at the aural test in grade exams!

0-571-53438-4	Grade 1 (with CD)
0-571-53439-2	Grade 2 (with CD)
0-571-53544-5	Grade 3 (with CD)
0-571-53545-3	Grade 4 (with CD)
0-571-53546-1	Grade 5 (with CD)
0-571-53440-6	Grade 6 (with CD)
0-571-53441-4	Grades 7–8 (with CD)

Improve your theory!

These brilliant theory workbooks take students through all areas of music theory covered by the ABRSM examinations (grades 1 to 5). Firmly rooted in Paul Harris's Simultaneous Learning approach, they help develop every aspect of musicianship through a series of practice questions, fun games and quizzes, activities that connect theory with pupils' own pieces, as well as opportunities for composing, improvising, aural and listening exercises. Never before has theory been so fun or seemed so natural!

0-571-53861-4 Grade 1
0-571-53862-2 Grade 2
0-571-53863-0 Grade 3
0-571-53864-9 Grade 4
0-571-53865-7 Grade 5

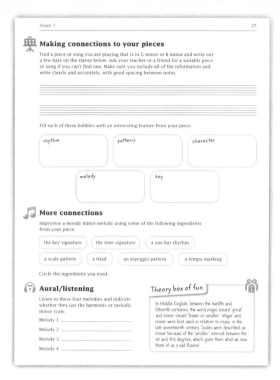

Improve your scales!

Paul Harris's *Improve your scales!* series is the best way to learn scales.

These workbooks contain not only the complete scales and arpeggios for the current ABRSM syllabus but also use finger fitness exercises, scale and arpeggio studies, key pieces and simple improvisations to help you play scales and arpeggios with real confidence.

This unique approach encourages the student to understand and play comfortably within in a key, thus helping them pick up those valuable extra marks in exams, as well as promoting a solid basis for the learning of repertoire and for sight-reading.

0-571-53411-2 Piano Grade 1
0-571-53412-0 Piano Grade 2
0-571-53413-9 Piano Grade 3
0-571-53414-7 Piano Grade 4
0-571-53415-5 Piano Grade 5

0-571-53701-4 Violin Grade 1
0-571-53702-2 Violin Grade 2
0-571-53703-0 Violin Grade 3
0-571-53704-9 Violin Grade 4
0-571-53705-7 Violin Grade 5

0-571-52024-3 Flute Grades 1–3
0-571-52025-1 Flute Grades 4–5

0-571-51475-8 Clarinet Grades 1–3
0-571-51476-6 Clarinet Grades 4–5

Improve your teaching!

These insightful volumes are distilled from years of personal experience and research. In his approachable style, Paul Harris outlines his innovative strategy of 'simultaneous learning' as well as offering advice on lesson preparation, aural and memory work, effective practice and more.

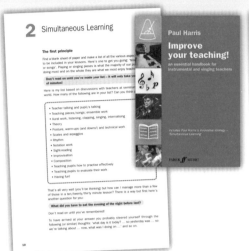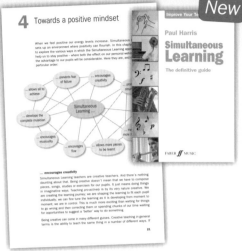

0-571-53868-1   Simultaneous Learning
0-571-52534-2   Improve your teaching!
0-571-53175-X   Teaching beginners
0-571-53676-X   The Virtuoso Teacher
0-571-53833-9   The Practice Process
0-571-53319-1   Group Music Teaching in Practice

Musicians' Union The Complete Practice Workbook and Musicians' Union Practice Diary

These two practice diaries are suitable for all instrumental and singing lessons. The *Musicians' Union Practice Diary* is a must-have, fun diary for young players. *The Complete Practice Workbook* is aimed at slightly older players and contains a Simultaneous Learning Practice Map for every lesson.

Simultaneous Learning Practice Map pad

This Practice Map pad is a revolutionary way to set up practice, based on the Simultaneous Learning approach.

0-571-59733-5 Musicians' Union Practice Diary
0-571-59734-3 Musicians' Union: The Complete Practice Workbook
0-571-59731-9 The Simultaneous Learning Practice Map Pad

Faber Music Ltd.
Burnt Mill
Elizabeth Way
Harlow
Essex
CM20 2HX

t   +44 (0)1279 828982
f   +44 (0)1279 828983
e   sales@fabermusic.com
w   www.fabermusicstore.com
    @fabermusic
f   facebook.com/fabermusic

Set 2: More leaps in D major

5

6

7

Set 3: More leaps in A major

8

9

10

Set 4: Both keys

11

12

13

Prepared pieces

> **1** What is the key? Play the scale and name all the notes.
>
> **2** What will you count? Tap the rhythm of the piece.
>
> **3** Find the two leaps. What do they have in common?
>
> **4** Think about how you will finger the piece.
>
> **5** How will you put some character into your performance?

1

> **1** How will you count this piece?
>
> **2** Do any bars contain the same rhythmic patterns?
>
> **3** Tap the rhythm then, tapping the pulse, hear the rhythm in your head.
>
> **4** How may leaps can you find? How will you finger them?
>
> **5** How will you put some character into your performance?

2

Improvising

1

> Make up your own piece (it can be as long or as short as you like), beginning with this pattern. Keep the pulse steady.
>
>

2

> Now make up your own piece in $\frac{3}{4}$, in D or A major.

Going solo!

Don't forget to prepare each piece carefully before you play it.

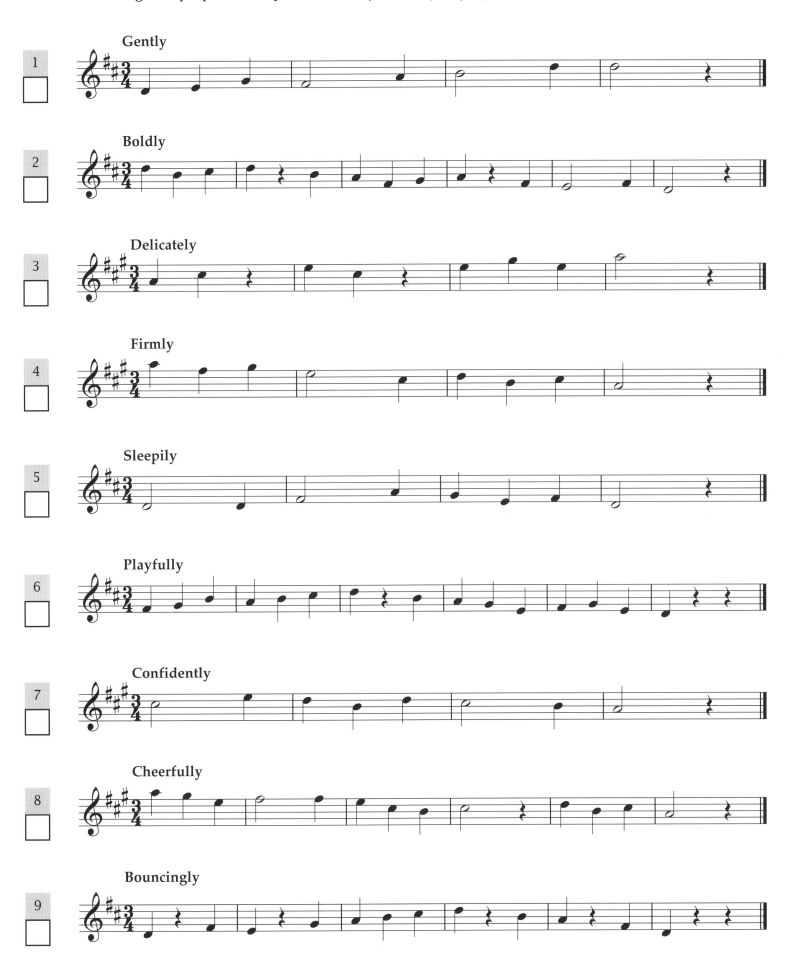

Stage 4

Rhythmic exercises

Always remember to count two bars in.

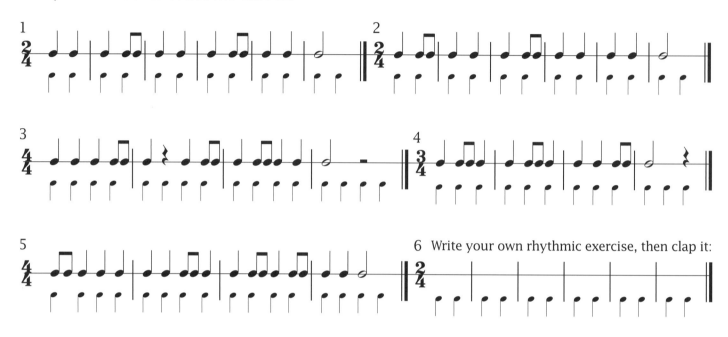

Melodic exercises

Set 1: Exploring quavers 1

Set 2: Exploring quavers 2

Set 4: Exploring dynamics 2

Prepared pieces

> **1** Explain the time signature of this piece.
>
> **2** Do any bars contain the same rhythmic patterns?
>
> **3** Clap the rhythm then, tapping the pulse, hear the rhythm in your head.
>
> **4** How will you put some character into your performance?
>
> **5** Play an A (the first note) then, tapping the pulse, hear the piece in your head.

1

> **1** What is the key? Play the scale with a dancing character.
>
> **2** Say the names of all the notes.
>
> **3** What will you count? Tap the rhythm of the piece.
>
> **4** What do the two dynamic markings tell you?
>
> **5** Play a D then hear the piece in your head, with the dynamics.

2

Improvising

1

Make up your own piece (it can be as long or as short as you like), beginning with this pattern. Keep the pulse steady.

2

Now make up your own piece which includes some dynamics.

Going solo!

Don't forget to prepare each piece carefully before you play it.

Stage 5

Here are some patterns you have already met in this book,
beginning on open D. Have your violin and fingers ready, and
look at each exercise for a couple of seconds. Then shut your
eyes and play it. Check to see if you were right. If you were,
you are already successfully reading patterns *at a glance*.

In the next exercises try to take in each 3-beat group at a glance
and, as you are playing, look ahead to the next group.

Prepared pieces

1 Why is it a good idea to read ahead?

2 How many different rhythm patterns can you find in each piece?

3 Tap the rhythm of each piece then, tapping the pulse, hear the rhythm in your head.

4 Try to hear the piece in your head before you play it.

5 Think about reading ahead before you begin each piece.

Going solo!

Don't forget to prepare each piece carefully before you play it.

Stage 6

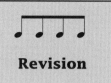

Rhythmic exercises

Melodic exercises

Going solo!

Don't forget to prepare each piece carefully before you play it.

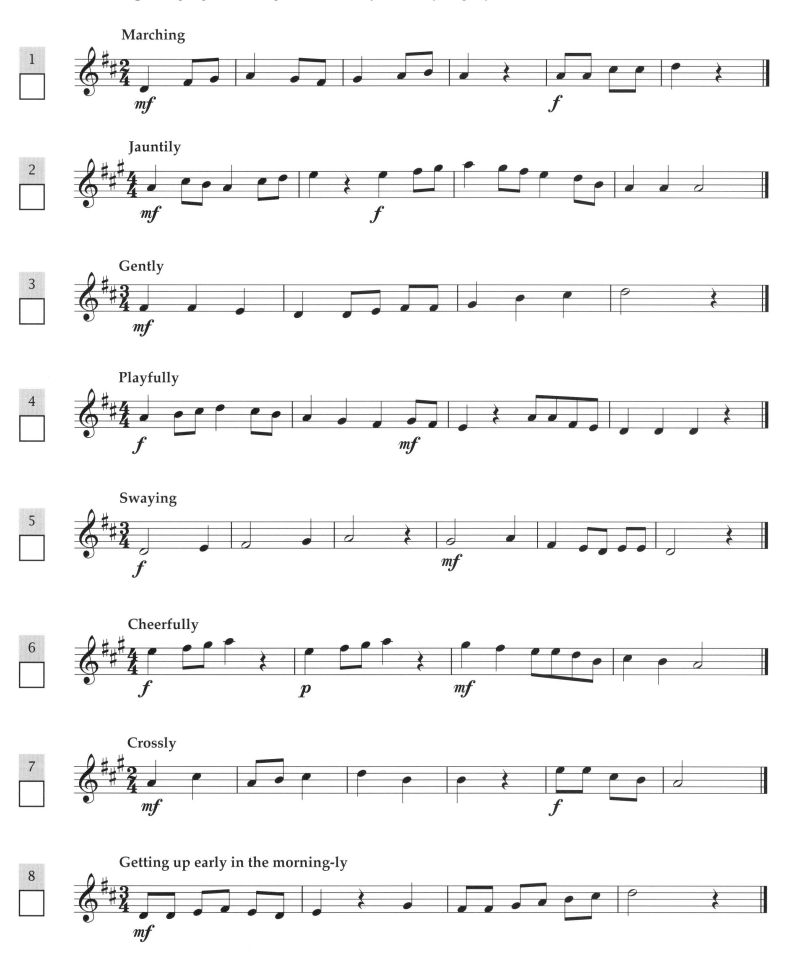